Family Teatime

Recipes, Tips & Treats
A Delicious Collection for Afternoon Tea

**FLAME TREE
PUBLISHING**

Contents

Introduction 4

Traditional Oven Scones 6

Types of Teatime 7

Scotch Pancakes 8

The Perfect Dinner Table 9

Fruity Apple Tea Bread.................................10

Maple, Pecan & Lemon Loaf 11

Lemon Drizzle Cake.......................................12

The Adventures of Alice in Wonderland 13

Teatime in England 14

Honey Cake 16

Lemon Bars 17

Swiss Roll..18

The Origin of Tea...19

Easy Victoria Sponge 20

Finger Sandwiches 21

Toffee Apple Cake 22

Iced Tea 23

Crunchy-Topped Citrus Chocolate Slices 24

Banana Cake 25

Carrot Cake 26

Fun Fact & Did You Know? 27

Chocolate Whirls 28

Tips for Baking Perfect Cookies 30

Chewy Chocolate & Nut Cookies 31

Keep It Clean 32

Whipped Shortbread 33

Fruit & Nut Flapjacks 34

Tea: a Social Drink 35

Canning Time 35

Ginger Snaps 37

Chocolate Chip Cherry Muffins 38

Teatime Etiquette 39

Natural Theology 40

Almond & Cherry Cupcakes 41

Coffee & Walnut Fudge Cupcakes 42

Polly Put the Kettle On 43

Fondant Fancies 44

Raspberry Butterfly Cupcakes 46

Chocolate & Toffee Cupcakes 47

Introduction

'... there are few hours in life more agreeable than the hour dedicated to the ceremony known as afternoon tea.'

from *The Portrait of a Lady*, chapter 1, by Henry James (1843–1916)

'Teatime' can be many things to many people. It is a beloved traditional treat designed for that time between lunch and dinner when you need something to stave off that peckish feeling – or it can be almost a meal in itself. A warm, soothing cup of tea and some delicious cake or a scone smothered with cream and jam is just the thing to hit the spot, and feels very civilized. From its origins in China, tea has travelled across the continents to become a refreshing and enjoyable social drink, and the addition of delectable food has evolved into the practice of teatime, a fun and pleasurable way to pass the time.

Little girls play at having tea parties with all the proper etiquette of a good hostess, tea rooms with their gleaming tiered stands of treats exist in high-end hotels, and quaint tea shops with their porcelain cups attract flocks of customers. Afternoon tea has a real charm about it and is a particularly enjoyable way to bring the family together, whether huddled by the fireplace in winter or outside enjoying the summer sun. Even the act of baking itself is something children can get involved with, making teatime even more special.

This lovely book provides a selection of delicious recipes for all the family, accompanied by a delightful mixture of fun facts, baking tips, poetry and everything you ever wanted to know about the evolution and practice of afternoon tea.

5

Traditional Oven Scones

Serves 8–10

Ingredients

225 g / 8 oz / 2 cups self-raising flour
1 tsp baking powder
pinch salt
40 g / 1½ oz / 3 tbsp butter, cubed
1 tbsp caster / superfine sugar
150 ml / ¼ pint / ⅔ cup milk,
    plus 1 tbsp for brushing
1 tbsp plain / all-purpose flour, to dust

Preheat the oven to 220°C/425°F/Gas Mark 7, 15 minutes before baking. Sift the self-raising flour, baking powder and salt into a large bowl. Rub in the butter until the mixture resembles fine breadcrumbs. Stir in the sugar and mix in enough milk to give a fairly soft dough.

Knead the dough on a lightly floured surface for a few seconds until smooth. Roll out until 2 cm/¾ inch thick and stamp out 6.5 cm/2½ inch rounds with a floured plain cutter. Place on an oiled baking sheet and brush the tops with milk – do not brush it over the sides or the scones will not rise properly. Dust with a little plain/all-purpose flour.

Bake in the oven for 12–15 minutes until well risen and golden brown. Transfer to a wire rack and serve warm or leave to cool completely. The scones are best eaten on the day of baking, but may be kept in an airtight container for up to two days.

Types of Teatime

Cream Tea: This consists of tea and scones with jam and cream.

Afternoon Tea: This can refer to a less formal cup of tea and a treat in the afternoon, and has evolved to refer to the delicious selection of sandwiches and sweet treats served in hotels and cafés in mid-afternoon. It has also been called 'Low Tea' because traditionally it was taken in a room with low tables placed near chairs. Other terms for afternoon tea include:

Light Tea: This is similar to a cream tea, but contains various sweets as well as scones.

Full Tea: This involves tea, sweets and savouries.

High Tea: More substantial than afternoon tea, this can include cold meats, eggs and fish in addition to the cakes and sandwiches, and is usually eaten later. This was traditionally taken by the lower and middle classes as one of their main meals.

Scotch Pancakes

Makes 18

Ingredients

white vegetable fat/shortening,
    for greasing
175 g / 6 oz / heaping 1⅓ cups
    self-raising flour
1 tsp baking powder
40 g / 1½ oz / scant ¼ cup
    caster / superfine sugar
1 medium / large egg
200 ml / 7 fl oz / 1 scant cup milk
butter, maple syrup or jam/jelly,
    to serve

Grease a heavy-based nonstick frying pan or a flat griddle pan with white vegetable fat/shortening and heat gently.

Sift the flour and baking powder into a bowl, stir in the sugar and make a well in the centre. Add the egg and half the milk and beat to a smooth thick batter. Beat in enough of the remaining milk to give the consistency of thick cream.

Drop the mixture onto the hot pan 1 heaped tablespoon at a time, spacing them well apart. When small bubbles rise to the surface of each scone, flip them over with a spatula and cook for about 1 minute until golden brown.

Place on a serving dish and keep warm, covered with a clean cloth, while you cook the remaining mixture. Serve with butter, syrup or jam/jelly.

The Perfect Dinner Table (extract)

Our manners may not be the best;
Perhaps our elbows often rest
Upon the table, and at times
That very worst of dinner crimes,
That very shameful act and rude
Of speaking ere you've downed your food,
Too frequently, I fear, is done,
So fast the little voices run.

by Edgar Albert Guest (1881–1959)

TEA TIME

Fruity Apple Tea Bread

Cuts into 12 slices

Ingredients

125 g / 4 oz / ½ cup (1 stick) butter
125 g / 4 oz / ⅔ cup soft light brown sugar
275 g / 10 oz / 2 cups sultanas / golden raisins
150 ml / ¼ pint / ⅔ cup apple juice
1 eating apple, peeled, cored and chopped
2 medium / large eggs, beaten
275 g / 10 oz / 2½ cups plain / all-purpose flour
½ tsp ground cinnamon
½ tsp ground ginger
2 tsp bicarbonate of soda / baking soda
butter curls, to serve

To decorate:
1 eating apple, cored and sliced
1 tsp lemon juice
1 tbsp golden syrup / light corn syrup, warmed

Preheat the oven to 180°C/350°F/Gas Mark 4. Oil and line the base of a 900 g/2 lb/9x5x3-inch loaf tin/pan. Put the butter, sugar, sultanas/golden raisins and apple juice in a small saucepan. Heat gently, stirring occasionally, until the butter has melted. Tip into a bowl and leave to cool.

Stir in the chopped apple and beaten eggs. Sift the flour, spices and bicarbonate of soda/baking soda over the apple mixture. Mix well and spoon into the loaf tin and smooth the top level. Toss the apple slices in lemon juice and arrange on top. Bake in the oven for 50 minutes, or until a skewer/toothpick inserted into the centre comes out clean. Cover with kitchen foil and leave in the tin for 10 minutes before turning out onto a wire rack to cool. Brush the top with golden/corn syrup and leave to cool. Remove the lining paper, cut into thick slices and serve with curls of butter.

Maple, Pecan & Lemon Loaf

Cuts into 12 slices

Ingredients

350 g / 12 oz / 2¾ cups plain /
    all-purpose flour
1 tsp baking powder
175 g / 6 oz / ¾ cup (1½ sticks) butter, cubed
75 g / 3 oz / ⅓ cup caster / superfine sugar
125 g / 4 oz / 1¼ cups roughly chopped
    pecan nuts
3 medium / large eggs
1 tbsp milk
finely grated zest of 1 lemon
5 tbsp maple syrup

For the icing:
75 g / 3 oz / ¾ cup icing / confectioners' sugar
1 tbsp lemon juice
25 g / 1 oz / ¼ cup roughly chopped pecans

Preheat the oven to 170°C/325°F/Gas Mark 3, 10 minutes before baking. Lightly oil and line the base of a 900 g/2 lb/9x5x3-inch loaf tin/pan with nonstick baking parchment. Sift the flour and baking powder into a large bowl. Rub in the butter until the mixture resembles fine breadcrumbs. Stir in the caster/superfine sugar and pecan nuts. Beat the eggs together with the milk and lemon zest. Stir in the maple syrup. Add to the dry ingredients and gently stir in until mixed thoroughly to make a soft dropping consistency.

Spoon the mixture into the tin and level the top. Bake in the oven for 50–60 minutes until the cake is well risen and lightly browned. Leave the cake in the tin for about 10 minutes, then turn out and leave to cool on a wire rack. Carefully remove the lining paper.

Sift the icing/confectioners' sugar into a small bowl and stir in the lemon juice to make a smooth icing. Drizzle the icing over the top of the loaf, then scatter with the chopped pecans. Leave to set, slice thickly and serve.

Lemon Drizzle Cake

Serves 8–10

Ingredients

125 g / 4 oz / ½ cup (1 stick) butter or margarine

175 g / 6 oz / heaping ¾ cup caster / superfine sugar

2 large / extra-large eggs

175 g / 6 oz / heaping 1½ cups self-raising flour

2 lemons, preferably unwaxed

50 g / 2 oz / ¼ cup granulated sugar

Preheat the oven to 180°C/350°F/Gas Mark 4, 10 minutes before baking. Lightly oil and line the base of an 18 cm/7 inch square cake tin/pan with baking parchment.

In a large bowl, cream the butter or margarine and caster/superfine sugar together until soft and fluffy.

Beat the eggs, then gradually add a little of the egg to the creamed mixture, adding 1 tablespoon of flour after each addition.

Finely grate the zest from 1 of the lemons and stir into the creamed mixture, beating well until smooth. Squeeze the juice from the lemon, strain, then stir into the mixture. Spoon into the prepared tin, level the surface and bake in the preheated oven for 25–30 minutes. Using a zester, remove the zest from the last lemon and mix with half of the granulated sugar and reserve.

Squeeze the juice into a small saucepan. Add the rest of the granulated sugar to the lemon juice in the saucepan and heat gently, stirring occasionally. When the sugar has dissolved, simmer gently for 3–4 minutes until syrupy.

With a cocktail stick or fine skewer, prick the cake all over. Sprinkle the lemon zest and sugar over the top of the cake, drizzle over the syrup and leave to cool in the tin. Cut the cake into squares and serve.

Top Tips

Whole lemons keep well for weeks in the fridge if you store them in egg cartons: the less air that circulates around a lemon, the longer it seems to keep.

Cut lemons last longer if you place them cut-side down on a plate or saucer and cover them with an inverted glass.

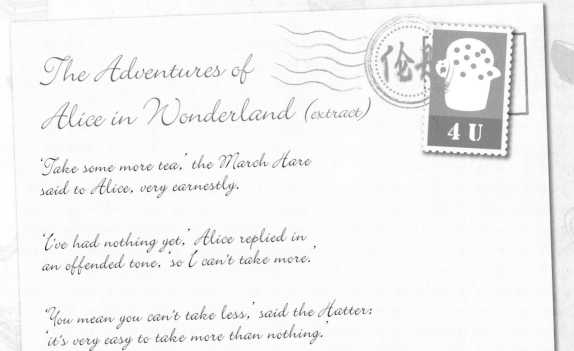

The Adventures of
Alice in Wonderland (extract)

'Take some more tea,' the March Hare
said to Alice, very earnestly.

'I've had nothing yet,' Alice replied in
an offended tone, 'so I can't take more.'

'You mean you can't take less,' said the Hatter:
'it's very easy to take more than nothing.'

from chapter 7, by Lewis Carroll (1832–1898)

Teatime in England

Catherine of Braganza, the Portuguese wife of King Charles II, is credited with making tea popular in England. As someone who loved tea, she made it popular in the English court, and then amongst the wealthy classes who were heavily influenced by royalty. Charles himself, who had lived in Europe before becoming King, was a tea drinker, and soon it became England's national drink – overtaking ale!

It was the Duchess of Bedford, in Queen Victoria's time, who is credited with introducing teatime to England. She grew hungry between the two meals of the day – lunch and dinner, thus she started inviting friends over in the afternoons to enjoy tea and cake, sandwiches and sweets.

瓦尼仑仑冗

15

Honey Cake

Cuts into 6 slices

Ingredients

50 g / 2 oz / 4 tbsp butter

2 tbsp caster / superfine sugar

125 g / 4 oz / ⅓ cup clear honey

175 g / 6 oz / heaping 1⅓ cups plain / all-purpose flour

½ tsp bicarbonate of soda / baking soda

½ tsp mixed / pumpkin pie spice

1 medium / large egg

2 tbsp milk

25 g / 1 oz / ¼ cup flaked almonds

1 tbsp clear honey, to drizzle

Preheat the oven to 180°C/350°F/Gas Mark 4, 10 minutes before baking. Lightly oil and line the base of an 18 cm/7 inch, deep round cake tin/pan with lightly oiled greaseproof/wax paper or baking parchment.

In a saucepan, gently heat the butter, sugar and honey until the butter has just melted. Sift the flour, bicarbonate of soda/baking soda and mixed/pumpkin pie spice together into a bowl. Beat the egg and the milk until mixed thoroughly.

Make a well in the centre of the sifted flour mixture and pour in the melted butter and honey. Using a wooden spoon, beat well, gradually drawing in the flour from the sides of the bowl.

When all the flour has been beaten in, add the egg mixture and mix thoroughly. Pour into the prepared tin and sprinkle with the flaked almonds. Bake in the preheated oven for 30–35 minutes until well risen and golden brown and a skewer/toothpick inserted into the centre of the cake comes out clean.

Remove from the oven, and cool for a few minutes in the tin before turning out and leaving to cool on a wire rack. Drizzle with the remaining tablespoon of honey and serve.

Lemon Bars

Makes 24

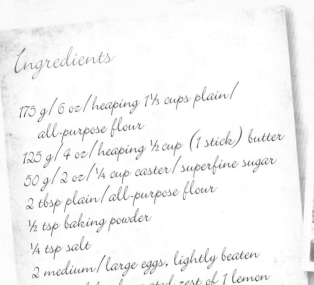

Ingredients

175 g / 6 oz / heaping 1⅓ cups plain /
  all-purpose flour
125 g / 4 oz / heaping ½ cup (1 stick) butter
50 g / 2 oz / ¼ cup caster / superfine sugar
2 tbsp plain / all-purpose flour
½ tsp baking powder
¼ tsp salt
2 medium / large eggs, lightly beaten
juice and finely grated zest of 1 lemon
sifted icing / confectioners' sugar, to decorate

Preheat the oven to 170°C/325°F/Gas Mark 3, 10 minutes before baking. Lightly oil and line a 20.5 cm/8 inch square cake tin/pan with greaseproof/wax paper or baking parchment.

Rub together the flour and butter until the mixture resembles breadcrumbs. Stir in 4 tablespoons of the caster/superfine sugar and mix. Turn the mixture into the prepared tin and press down firmly. Bake in the oven for 20 minutes until pale golden.

Meanwhile, in a food processor, mix together the remaining sugar, the flour, baking powder, salt, eggs, lemon juice and zest until smooth. Pour over the prepared base.

Transfer to the oven and bake for a further 20–25 minutes until nearly set but still a bit wobbly in the centre. Remove from the oven and cool in the tin on a wire rack. Dust with icing/confectioners' sugar and cut into squares. Serve cold and store in an airtight container.

Swiss Roll

Cuts into 8 slices

Ingredients

75 g / 3 oz / ⅔ cup self-raising flour
3 large / extra-large eggs
1 tsp vanilla extract
100 g / 3½ oz / ½ cup caster /
  superfine sugar
25 g / 1 oz / ¼ cup toasted
  and finely chopped hazelnuts
3 tbsp apricot jam / jelly
300 ml / ½ pint / 1¼ cups double /
  heavy cream, lightly whipped

Preheat the oven to 220°C/425°F/Gas Mark 7, 15 minutes before baking.
Lightly oil and line the base of a 23 x 33 cm/9 x 13 inch Swiss roll tin/jelly roll pan
with a single sheet of greaseproof/wax paper or baking parchment. Sift the flour several
times, then set on top of the oven to warm a little.

Place a mixing bowl with the eggs, vanilla extract and sugar over a saucepan of hot water,
ensuring that the base of the bowl is not touching the water. With the saucepan off the heat,
whisk with an electric hand whisk until the egg mixture becomes pale and mousse-like and
has increased in volume.

Remove the basin from the saucepan and continue to whisk for a further 2–3 minutes. Sift in
the flour and very gently fold in, trying not to knock out the air already whisked in. Pour

into the tin, tilting to ensure that the mixture is evenly distributed.
Bake in the oven for 10–12 minutes until well risen, golden brown and the top springs back when touched lightly with a finger.

Sprinkle the toasted, chopped hazelnuts over a large sheet of greaseproof/wax paper. When the cake has cooked, turn out onto the hazelnut-covered paper and trim the edges of the cake. Holding an edge of the paper with the short side of the cake nearest you, roll the cake up. When fully cold, carefully unroll and spread with the jam/jelly and then the cream. Roll back up and serve. Otherwise, store in the refrigerator and eat within two days.

The Origin of Tea

According to legend, the first instance of tea drinking came about by accident. In 2737 BC, Emperor Shen Nong of China was travelling when he asked his servants to boil some water by the roadside - to purify it for drinking. Whilst they were doing this, leaves from a nearby tree fell into the water, and the Emperor decided to try the resulting concoction. He enjoyed the drink so much, he asked them to make more. The leaves were of course from the Camellia sinensis tree - the plant which gives us tea.

Easy Victoria Sponge

Serves 8–10

Ingredients

225 g / 8 oz / 1 cup soft margarine
225 g / 8 oz / heaping 1 cup caster / superfine sugar
4 medium / large eggs
1 tsp vanilla extract
225 g / 8 oz / 1¾ cups self-raising flour
1 tsp baking powder
icing / confectioners' sugar, to dust

For the filling:
4 tbsp seedless raspberry jam / jelly
100 ml / 3½ fl oz / scant ½ cup double / heavy cream

Did you know?

The Victoria Sponge was named after Queen Victoria, who enjoyed a slice with her tea in the afternoon.

Preheat the oven to 180°C/350°F/Gas Mark 4. Grease two 20.5 cm/8 inch sandwich tins/layer cake pans and line the bases with nonstick baking parchment.

Place the margarine, sugar, eggs and vanilla extract in a large bowl and sift in the flour and baking powder. Beat for about 2 minutes until smooth and blended, then divide between the tins and smooth level.

Bake for about 25 minutes until golden, well risen and the tops of the cakes spring back when lightly touched with a fingertip. Leave to cool in the tins for 2 minutes, then turn out onto a wire rack to cool. When cool, peel away the baking parchment.

When completely cold, spread one cake with jam/jelly and place on a serving plate. Whip the cream until it forms soft peaks, then spread on the underside of the other cake. Sandwich the two cakes together and sift a little icing/confectioners' sugar over the top.

Finger Sandwiches

Another common teatime treat is finger sandwiches, traditionally quite dainty but still delicious!

Typically teatime finger sandwiches are small and thinly sliced – usually cut into small squares or triangles (cutting one regular sandwich into four), and with the crusts removed. You can even try cutting your sandwiches into fun and interesting shapes with cookie cutters.

These sandwiches might be small, but they are designed to be packed with flavour. They can be prepared with various dressings, and to prevent them from going soggy they should be spread with butter or cream cheese.

Suggested fillings:

Cucumber
Smoked salmon
Cream cheese
Egg and cress
Ham and mustard

Toffee Apple Cake

Cuts into 6–8 slices

Ingredients

2 small eating apples, peeled
50 g / 2 oz / ¼ cup soft dark brown sugar
175 g / 6 oz / ¾ cup (1½ sticks) butter
    or margarine
175 g / 6 oz / 1 scant cup caster / superfine sugar
3 medium / large eggs
175 g / 6 oz / heaping 1⅓ cup self-raising flour
150 ml / ¼ pint / ⅔ cup double / heavy cream
2 tbsp icing / confectioners' sugar
½ tsp vanilla extract
½ tsp ground cinnamon

Top Tip

You will find it easier to whip cream if the bowl and utensils are really cold, but, if the cream will not whip into shape, add 1 or 2 drops lemon juice to stiffen it.

Preheat the oven to 180°C/350°F/Gas Mark 4, 10 minutes before baking. Lightly oil and line the bases of two 20.5 cm/8 inch sandwich tins/layer cake pans with greaseproof/wax paper or baking parchment. Thinly slice the apples, toss them in the brown sugar and arrange in the prepared tins. Reserve.

Cream together the butter or margarine and caster/superfine sugar until light and fluffy. Beat the eggs together in a small bowl. Gradually beat them into the creamed mixture, beating well between each addition. Sift the flour into the mixture and fold in. Divide the mixture between the two cake tins and level the surface. Bake in the oven for 25–30 minutes until golden and well risen. Leave to cool.

Lightly whip the cream with 1 tablespoon of the icing/confectioners' sugar and the vanilla extract. Sandwich the cakes together with the cream. Mix the remaining icing sugar and the ground cinnamon together, sprinkle over the top of the cake and serve.

Iced Tea

A refreshing way to have your tea is to have it cold – particularly good during the summer months!

To make iced tea:

Leave tea bags or tea leaves in a jug of cold water to steep in a refrigerator overnight, then strain and pour over ice cubes into a glass.

You can even mix in syrup, fruit juice or chopped fruit before serving for different variations.

Top Tip

Make ice cubes out of your tea to stop your drink from becoming diluted.

Crunchy-Topped Citrus Chocolate Slices

Makes 12 slices

Ingredients

175 g / 6 oz / ¾ cup (1½ sticks) butter
175 g / 6 oz / ¾ cup firmly packed
   muscovado / dark brown sugar
finely grated zest of 1 orange
3 medium / large eggs, lightly beaten
1 tbsp ground almonds
175 g / 6 oz / heaping 1⅓ cups self-raising flour
¼ tsp baking powder
125 g / 4 oz dark / semisweet dark chocolate,
   coarsely grated
2 tsp milk

For the crunchy topping:
125 g / 4 oz / ⅔ cup caster / superfine sugar
juice of 2 limes
juice of 1 orange

Preheat the oven to 170°C/325°F/Gas Mark 3, 10 minutes before baking. Oil and line a 28 x 18 x 2.5 cm/11 x 7 x 1 inch cake tin/pan with nonstick baking parchment. Place the butter, sugar and orange zest into a large bowl and cream together until light and fluffy. Gradually add the eggs, beating after each addition, then beat in the ground almonds. Sift the flour and baking powder into the creamed mixture. Add the grated chocolate and milk, then gently fold in using a metal spoon. Spoon the mixture into the tin.

Bake in the oven for 35–40 minutes until well risen and firm to the touch. Leave in the tin for a few minutes to cool slightly. Turn out onto a wire rack and remove the lining paper.

For the topping, place the sugar and fruit juices into a small jug. Stir together. Drizzle over the hot cake, covering the whole surface. Leave until completely cold, then cut into slices to serve.

Banana Cake

Cuts into 8 slices

Ingredients

3 medium-sized ripe bananas

1 tsp lemon juice

150 g / 5 oz / ¾ cup brown sugar

75 g / 3 oz / 6 tbsp butter or margarine

250 g / 9 oz / 2 cups self-raising flour

1 tsp ground cinnamon

3 medium / large eggs

50 g / 2 oz / ⅓ cup chopped walnuts

1 tsp each ground cinnamon and
    caster / superfine sugar

fresh cream, to serve

Preheat the oven to 190°C/375°F/Gas Mark 5, 10 minutes before baking. Lightly oil and line the base of an 18 cm/7 inch deep round cake tin/pan with greaseproof/wax paper or baking parchment. Mash two of the bananas in a small bowl, sprinkle with the lemon juice and a heaped tablespoon of the brown sugar. Mix together lightly and reserve.

Gently heat the remaining brown sugar and butter or margarine in a small saucepan until the butter has just melted. Pour into a small bowl, then allow to cool slightly. Sift the flour and cinnamon into a large bowl and make a well in the centre.

Beat the eggs into the cooled sugar mixture, pour into the well of flour and mix thoroughly. Gently stir in the mashed banana mixture. Pour half of the mixture into the tin. Thinly slice the remaining banana and arrange over the cake mixture. Sprinkle over the chopped walnuts, then cover with the remaining cake mixture.

Bake in the oven for 50–55 minutes until well risen and golden brown. Allow to cool in the tin, turn out and sprinkle with the ground cinnamon and caster/superfine sugar. Serve hot or cold with a jug of fresh cream for pouring.

Carrot Cake

Cuts into 8 slices

Ingredients

200 g / 7 oz / 1⅔ cups plain / all-purpose flour

½ tsp ground cinnamon

½ tsp freshly grated nutmeg

1 tsp baking powder

1 tsp bicarbonate of soda / baking soda

150 g / 5 oz / ¾ cup dark muscovado / brown sugar

200 ml / 7 fl oz / ¾ cup vegetable oil

3 medium / large eggs

225 g / 8 oz / 2 cups peeled and roughly grated carrots

50 g / 2 oz / ½ cup chopped walnuts

For the frosting:

175 g / 6 oz / ¾ cup cream cheese

finely grated zest of 1 orange

1 tbsp orange juice

1 tsp vanilla extract

125 g / 4 oz / 1 cup icing / confectioners' sugar

Preheat the oven to 150°C/300°F/Gas Mark 2, 10 minutes before baking. Lightly oil and line the base of a 15 cm/ 6 inch deep square cake tin/pan with greaseproof/wax paper or baking parchment.

Sift the flour, spices, baking powder and bicarbonate of soda/baking soda together into a large bowl. Stir in the dark muscovado/brown sugar and mix together.

Lightly whisk the oil and eggs together, then gradually stir into the flour and sugar mixture. Stir well. Add the carrots and walnuts. Mix thoroughly, then pour into the prepared cake tin.

Bake in the oven for 1¼ hours, or until light and springy to the touch and a skewer inserted into the centre of the cake comes out clean. Remove from the oven and allow to cool in the tin for 5 minutes before turning out onto a wire rack. Reserve until cold.

For the frosting, beat together the cream cheese, orange zest, orange juice and vanilla extract. Sift the icing/confectioners' sugar and stir into the cream cheese mixture. When the cake is cold, discard the lining paper, spread the frosting over the top and serve cut into squares.

Fun Fact

In the nineteenth century, moustaches were all the rage – so much so that 'moustache cups' were invented. These were tea cups with a little ledge inside to prevent men from getting their moustache wet whilst sipping their tea!

Did You Know?

The first book about tea was written by Lu Yu (c. 800 AD). It was called Tea Classic and discussed every aspect of tea, from its history and geography to the method of brewing perfect tea and even how to drink it.

Chocolate Whirls

Makes 20

Ingredients

125 g / 4 oz / ½ cup (8 tbsp) soft margarine
75 g / 3 oz / 6 tbsp unsalted butter, softened
75 g / 3 oz / ¾ cup icing / confectioners' sugar, sifted
75 g / 3 oz dark / semisweet dark chocolate,
    melted and cooled
2 tbsp cornflour / cornstarch, sifted
125 g / 4 oz / 1 cup plain / all-purpose flour
125 g / 4 oz / 1 cup self-raising flour

For the buttercream:
125 g / 4 oz / ½ cup (1 stick) unsalted
    butter, softened
½ tsp vanilla extract
225 g / 8 oz / 2¼ cups icing / confectioners' sugar, sifted

Preheat the oven to 180°C/350°F/Gas Mark 4, 10 minutes before baking. Lightly oil two baking sheets. Cream the margarine, butter and icing/confectioners' sugar together until the mixture is light and fluffy.

Stir the chocolate until smooth, then beat into the creamed mixture. Stir in the cornflour/ cornstarch. Sift the flours together, then gradually add to the creamed mixture, a little at a time, beating well between each addition. Put the mixture in a piping bag fitted with a large star nozzle/tip and pipe 40 small whirls onto the baking sheets. Bake in the oven for 12–15 minutes until firm to the touch. Remove from the oven and leave to cool for about 2 minutes. Transfer the whirls to wire racks and leave to cool.

For the buttercream, cream the butter with the vanilla extract until soft. Gradually beat in the icing sugar and add a little cooled boiled water, if necessary, to give a smooth consistency. When the whirls are cold, pipe or spread on the butter cream, sandwich together and serve.

Tips for Baking Perfect Cookies

- Assemble all the ingredients before starting to bake, and measure them carefully.

- Switch the oven on at least 10 minutes before baking in order for it to reach the correct temperature. An oven thermometer is an excellent investment, as is a timer.

- Have the ingredients at room temperature and once the dough is made, depending on how soft it is, wrap and chill for 30 minutes or until firm.

- Do not use excessive flour when rolling out. This will destroy the balance of ingredients and give a poor result, which can be tough and heavy to eat.

- If using one baking sheet, place in the centre of the oven once the oven has reached the correct temperature. If using two, place the oven racks so that there is the same amount of space between them. If necessary switch the trays around during baking so that an even browning is achieved.

- Allow cooked cookies or biscuits to cool for a few minutes before attempting to remove them from the baking sheet, otherwise they could easily break up. Then, use a large spatula to transfer them to a wire cooling rack. Once on the cooling rack, press the tops down lightly with the back of the spatula to flatten.

Chewy Chocolate & Nut Cookies

Makes 18

Ingredients

15 g / ½ oz / 1 tbsp butter
4 medium / large egg whites
350 g / 12 oz / 3 cups icing /
   confectioners' sugar
75 g / 3 oz / ¾ cup cocoa powder
   (unsweetened)
2 tbsp plain / all-purpose flour
1 tsp instant coffee powder
125 g / 4 oz / 1 cup finely
   chopped walnuts

Preheat the oven to 180°C/350°F/Gas Mark 4, 10 minutes before baking. Lightly grease several baking sheets with the butter. Line with a sheet of nonstick baking parchment. Place the egg whites in a large, grease-free bowl. Whisk with an electric mixer until very frothy.

Add the sugar, cocoa powder, flour and coffee powder. Whisk again until the ingredients are blended thoroughly. Add 1 tablespoon water and continue to whisk on the highest speed until the mixture is very thick. Fold in the chopped walnuts.

Place tablespoons of the mixture onto the baking sheets, leaving plenty of space between them to allow them to expand during cooking. Bake in the oven for 12–15 minutes until the tops are firm, golden and quite cracked. Leave to cool for 30 seconds, then, using a spatula, transfer to a wire rack and leave to cool. Store in an airtight container.

Keep It Clean

Tea- and coffee-stained cups and mugs can be restored by scrubbing with equal parts vinegar and salt followed by a rinse in warm water.

Cloudy glasses can be made clear again if you soak them for 10–15 minutes in a solution of equal parts hot water and white vinegar and scrub with a soft bottle brush.

Use a paste of bicarbonate of soda/baking soda and water to remove tea and coffee stains from ceramic and melamine cups. Leave the solution in the cup for a while, then rub and rinse. So much more ecological than bleach, and it doesn't leave an aftertaste.

Make your dinner service sparkle by adding a splash of white vinegar to your rinse water or dishwater.

Whipped Shortbread

Makes 36

Ingredients

225 g / 8 oz / 1 cup (2 sticks)
   butter, softened
125 g / 4 oz / 1 cup icing /
   confectioners' sugar
175 g / 6 oz / heaping 1⅓ cups
   plain / all-purpose flour
hundreds and thousands / sprinkles
sugar strands
chocolate drops
silver balls
2–3 tsp lemon juice

Preheat the oven to 180°C/350°F/Gas Mark 4, 10 minutes before baking. Lightly oil a baking sheet. Cream the butter and 75 g/3 oz/⅔ cup of the icing/confectioners' sugar until fluffy. Gradually add the flour and continue beating for a further 2–3 minutes until it is smooth and light.

Spoon the mixture into a piping bag fitted with a large star nozzle/tip and pipe swirls onto the baking sheet. Keep the other half plain. Bake in the oven for 6–8 minutes until the bottoms are lightly browned. Remove from the oven and transfer to a wire rack to cool.

Sift the remaining icing sugar into a small bowl. Add the lemon juice and blend until a smooth icing forms. Using a small spoon, swirl the icing over half of the cooled cookies. Decorate with hundreds and thousands sprinkles, chocolate drops or silver balls and serve.

Fruit & Nut Flapjacks

Makes 12

Ingredients

75 g / 3 oz / 6 tbsp butter or margarine

125 g / 4 oz / ⅔ cup soft light brown sugar

3 tbsp golden / light corn syrup

50 g / 2 oz / ⅓ cup raisins

50 g / 2 oz / ½ cup roughly chopped walnuts

175 g / 6 oz / 2⅓ cups rolled oats

50 g / 2 oz / ½ cup icing / confectioners' sugar

1–1½ tbsp lemon juice

Preheat the oven to 180°C/350°F/Gas Mark 4, 10 minutes before baking. Lightly oil a 23 cm/9 inch square cake tin/pan.

Melt the butter or margarine with the sugar and syrup in a small saucepan over a low heat. Remove from the heat.

Stir the raisins, walnuts and oats into the syrup mixture and mix together well. Spoon evenly into the tin and press down well. Transfer to the oven and bake for 20–25 minutes. Remove from the oven and leave to cool in the tin. Cut into bars while still warm.

Sift the icing/confectioners' sugar into a small bowl, then gradually beat in the lemon juice a little at a time to form a thin icing. Place into an icing bag fitted with a writing nozzle/tip, then pipe thin lines over the flapjacks. Allow to cool and serve.

Tea: A Social Drink

The practice of afternoon tea became a social craze, particularly for the upper classes, in the late 1800s in England and America. High-class hotels such as the Ritz and the Plaza offered special rooms for people to meet and have afternoon tea and chat. Soon tea dances held in the afternoon also became a popular social event, and were often run by hotels.

Canning Time (extract)

I'm a-sittin' here an' dreamin'
Of the kettles that are steamin',
And the cares that have been troublin'
All have vanished in the bubblin'.

by Edgar Albert Guest (1881–1959)

Ginger Snaps

Makes 40

Ingredients

300 g / 11 oz / 1⅓ cups (2¾ sticks) butter or margarine, softened

225 g / 8 oz / heaping 1 cup demerara / turbinado (raw) sugar

3 tbsp black treacle / molasses

1 medium / large egg

400 g / 14 oz / heaping 3 cups plain / all-purpose flour

2 tsp bicarbonate of soda / baking soda

½ tsp salt

1 tsp ground ginger

1 tsp ground cloves

1 tsp ground cinnamon

50 g / 2 oz / ¼ cup caster / superfine sugar

Preheat the oven to 190°C/375°F/Gas Mark 5, 10 minutes before baking. Lightly oil a baking sheet. Cream together the butter or margarine and the sugar until light and fluffy. Warm the treacle/molasses in the microwave for 30–40 seconds, then add gradually to the butter mixture with the egg. Beat until well combined.

In a separate bowl, sift the flour, bicarbonate of soda/baking soda, salt, ground ginger, ground cloves and ground cinnamon. Add to the butter mixture and mix together to form a firm dough. Chill in the refrigerator for 1 hour. Shape the dough into small balls and roll in the caster/superfine sugar. Place well apart on the baking sheet.

Sprinkle the baking sheet with a little water and transfer to the oven. Bake for 12 minutes, or until golden and crisp. Transfer to a wire rack to cool and serve.

Chocolate Chip Cherry Muffins

Makes 12

Ingredients

75 g / 3 oz / ⅓ cup glacé / candied cherries

75 g / 3 oz milk or dark / semisweet dark chocolate chips

75 g / 3 oz / 6 tbsp soft margarine

200 g / 7 oz / 1 cup caster / superfine sugar

2 medium / large eggs

150 ml / ¼ pint / ⅔ cup thickset natural yogurt

5 tbsp milk

275 g / 10 oz / 2¼ cups plain / all-purpose flour

1 tsp bicarbonate of soda / baking soda

Preheat the oven to 200°C/400°F/Gas Mark 6. Line a 12-hole muffin tray/pan with deep paper cases. Wash and dry the cherries. Chop them roughly, mix them with the chocolate chips and set aside.

Beat the margarine and sugar together, then whisk in the eggs, yogurt and milk. Sift in the flour and bicarbonate of soda/baking soda. Stir until just combined.

Fold in three quarters of the cherries and chocolate chips. Spoon the mixture into the cases, filling them two-thirds full. Sprinkle the remaining cherries and chocolate chips over the top.

Bake for about 20 minutes until golden and firm. Leave in the tin for 4 minutes, then turn out to cool on a wire rack.

Teatime Etiquette

- Avoid leaving lipstick stains on your teacup by dabbing your mouth with your napkin before drinking.

- It is not necessary to extend your little finger whilst drinking from your cup, unless it naturally does so.

- If you have to leave the table, place your napkin on your seat whilst you are gone.

- When eating scones or cake, take polite, small bites, no matter how delicious they might be!

- If you are given a tea bag and hot water, resist the urge to dunk your teabag, but simply leave it for five minutes before removing.

Natural Theology (extract)

We had a kettle; we let it leak:
Our not repairing made it worse.
We haven't had any tea for a week...
The bottom is out of the Universe.

by Rudyard Kipling (1865–1936)

Top Tip

*If you want to stop fruit or nuts from sinking in
your cake batter, dust them with flour first.*

Almond and Cherry Cupcakes

Makes 12

Ingredients

50 g / 2 oz / ¼ cup glacé / candied cherries,
    plus extra for decoration
125 g / 4 oz / 1 cup self-raising flour,
    plus extra for dusting
125 g / 4 oz / ½ cup (8 tbsp) soft margarine
125 g / 4 oz / ⅔ cup caster / superfine sugar
2 medium / large eggs
½ tsp almond extract

To decorate:
125 g / 4 oz / 1 cup icing / confectioners' sugar
1 tsp lemon juice
pink food colouring

Preheat the oven to 190°C/375°F/Gas Mark 5. Line a 12-hole muffin tray/pan with small paper cases. Wash the cherries, then dry them thoroughly. Chop the cherries, then dust lightly in flour and set aside.

Sift the flour into a bowl, then add the margarine, sugar, eggs and extract. Beat until smooth for about 2 minutes, then fold in the chopped cherries.

Spoon into the paper cases. Bake for 15–20 minutes until golden and springy in the centre. Turn out to cool on a wire rack.

To decorate, mix the icing/confectioners' sugar with the lemon juice and 2 teaspoons water to form a smooth icing. Add a little pink food colouring and drizzle over the top of each cupcake. Place a halved cherry on top and leave to set for 30 minutes.

Coffee & Walnut Fudge Cupcakes

Makes 16–18

125 g / 4 oz / 1 cup self-raising flour
125 g / 4 oz / ½ cup (1 stick) butter, softened
125 g / 4 oz / ½ cup golden caster /
  unbleached sugar
2 medium / large eggs
1 tbsp golden / light corn syrup
50 g / 2 oz / ½ cup finely chopped walnuts

To decorate:
225 g / 8 oz / 1¼ cups golden icing /
  unbleached confectioners' sugar
125 g / 4 oz / ½ cup (1 stick) unsalted
  butter, at room temperature
2 tsp coffee extract
16–18 small walnut pieces

Preheat the oven to 200°C/400°F/Gas Mark 6. Line two 12-hole muffin trays/pans with 16–18 small foil cases, depending on the depth of the tray holes/cups.

Sift the flour into a bowl and add the butter, sugar, eggs and syrup. Beat for about 2 minutes, then fold in the walnuts.

Spoon the mixture into the paper cases and bake for about 12–14 minutes until well risen and springy in the centre. Remove to a wire rack to cool.

For the frosting, sift the icing/confectioners' sugar into a bowl. Add the butter, coffee extract and 1 tablespoon hot water. Beat until light and fluffy, then place in a piping bag fitted with a star nozzle/tip. Pipe a swirl on each cupcake and top with a walnut piece.

Polly Put the Kettle On

Polly put the kettle on,
Polly put the kettle on,
Polly put the kettle on,
We'll all have tea.

Sukey take it off again,
Sukey take it off again,
Sukey take it off again,
They've all gone away.

Author Unknown

It is said that the author of the nursery rhyme 'Polly Put the Kettle On' wrote it after watching his five children at play. When the girls wanted to play without their brothers they used to pretend to have a tea party, telling one daughter Polly to 'put the kettle on'. Once the brothers had gone off, they could tell another daughter Susan (Sukey) to 'take it off again'.

Fondant Fancies

Makes 16–18

Ingredients

150 g / 5 oz / 1¼ cups self-raising flour
150 g / 5 oz / ¾ cup caster / superfine sugar
50 g / 2 oz / ½ cup ground almonds
150 g / 5 oz / ⅔ cup (1¼ sticks)
    butter, softened
3 medium / large eggs, beaten
4 tbsp milk

To decorate:
450 g / 1 lb / 3¾ cups fondant icing sugar /
    pouring fondant confectioners' sugar
paste food colourings
selection fancy cake decorations

Preheat the oven to 180°C/350°F/Gas Mark 4. Line two 12-hole muffin trays/pans with 16–18 paper cases, depending on the depth of the holes.

Sift the flour into a bowl and stir in the caster/superfine sugar and almonds. Add the butter, eggs and milk and beat until smooth.

Spoon into the paper cases and bake for 15–20 minutes until golden and firm to the touch. Turn out to cool on a wire rack. When cool, trim the tops flat if they have peaked slightly.

To decorate, make the icing to a thick coating consistency by mixing the icing/confectioners' sugar with 1–2 tablespoons of warm water. Divide into batches and colour each separately with a little paste food colouring. Keep each bowl covered with a damp cloth until needed. Spoon some icing over each cupcake, being sure to flood it right to the edge. Top each with a fancy decoration and leave to set for 30 minutes.

45

Raspberry Butterfly Cupcakes

Makes 12–14

Ingredients

125 g / 4 oz / ⅔ cup caster / superfine sugar
125 g / 4 oz / ½ cup (8 tbsp) soft margarine
2 medium / large eggs
125 g / 4 oz / 1 cup self-raising flour
½ tsp baking powder
½ tsp vanilla extract

To decorate:

4 tbsp seedless raspberry jam / jelly
12–14 fresh raspberries
icing / confectioners' sugar, to dust

Preheat the oven to 190°C/375°F/Gas Mark 5. Line one or two muffin trays/pans with 12–14 paper cases, depending on the depth of the holes.

Place all the cupcake ingredients in a large bowl and beat with an electric mixer for about 2 minutes until smooth. Fill the paper cases halfway up with the mixture.

Bake for about 15 minutes until firm, risen and golden. Remove to a wire rack to cool. When cold, cut a small circle out of the top of each cupcake and then cut the circle in half to form wings.

Fill each cupcake with a teaspoon of raspberry jam/jelly. Replace the wings at an angle and top each with a fresh raspberry. Dust lightly with icing/confectioners' sugar and serve immediately.

Chocolate &
Toffee Cupcakes

Makes 12–14

Ingredients

125 g / 4 oz soft fudge
125 g / 4 oz / ½ cup (8 tbsp) soft margarine
125 g / 4 oz / ½ cup golden caster/
   unbleached superfine sugar
150 g / 5 oz / 1¼ cups self-raising flour
2 tbsp cocoa powder (unsweetened)
2 medium/large eggs
1 tbsp golden/light corn syrup

To decorate:
50 g / 2 oz / 4 tbsp unsalted butter, softened
300 g / 11 oz / 2½ cups icing/
   confectioners' sugar, sifted
flavouring of choice
food colourings
125 g / 4 oz / ½ cup full-fat cream cheese

Preheat the oven to 180°C/350°F/Gas Mark 4. Line one or two muffin trays/pans with 12–14 paper cases, depending on the depth of the holes. Cut one quarter of the fudge into slices for decoration. Chop the rest into small cubes. Set all the fudge aside.

Place the margarine and the sugar in a large bowl and then sift in the flour and cocoa powder. In another bowl, beat the eggs with the syrup, then add to the flour mixture. Whisk together until smooth. Gently fold in the fudge cubes.

Spoon the mixture into the cases, filling them three-quarters full. Bake for about 15 minutes until a skewer/toothpick inserted into the centre comes out clean. Turn out to cool on a wire rack.

For the frosting, beat the butter and icing sugar together until light and fluffy. Add flavourings and colourings of choice and beat again. Add the cream cheese and whisk until light and fluffy. Do not over-beat, however, as the mixture can become runny. Swirl over each cupcake, then top with a fudge slice.

Notes on the recipes:

Please note that the measurements provided in this book are presented as 'metric/imperial/US-cups' practical equivalents; certain food and cooking items that are termed differently in the UK and in North America are presented as 'UK term/US term'; and eggs are medium (UK)/large (US) and large (UK)/extra-large (US).

Publisher's Note:

Raw or semicooked eggs should not be consumed by babies, toddlers, pregnant or breast-feeding women, the elderly or people with a chronic illness.

Publisher & Creative Director: Nick Wells
Senior Project Editor: Catherine Taylor
Editorial: Laura Bulbeck
Art Director: Mike Spender
Layout Design: Jane Ashley
Digital Design & Production: Chris Herbert

Special thanks to Digby Smith and Helen Wall.

First published 2011 by
FLAME TREE PUBLISHING
Crabtree Hall, Crabtree Lane
Fulham, London SW6 6TY
United Kingdom
www.flametreepublishing.com

Flame Tree is part of The Foundry Creative Media Company Limited

A copy of the CIP data for this book is available from the British Library.

Picture Credits

All images courtesy of Foundry Arts except for the following, which are © Fine Art Photographic Library:
9 Joseph Clark (1834–1926), *Favourite Fruits*; 14 George Sheridan Knowles (1863–1931), *A Tea Party*; 15 Harold Piffard (1868–1939), *A Riverside Picnic*; 23 Thomas James Lloyd (1849–1910), *Tea in the Garden*; 27 Edward George Handel Lucas (1861–1936), *Silent Advocates of Temperance*, 1891; 29 artist unknown, *A Summer Tea Party*, c. 1900; 32 Edward George Handel Lucas (1861–1936), *Teetotallers*, 1897; 39 Harry Brooker (1848–1941), *Breakfast Time*; 43 artist unknown, *Best Wishes for the Little Ones*; 45 Thomas Webster (1800–1886), *A Birthday Tea-Party*, 1876 and courtesy of Shutterstock:
7 © Robyn Mackenzie; 21 © Simone van den Berg; 40 © studiogi
recurring decorations: © waterlilly; © Naci Yavuz; © Nikiparonak; © asel; © Woodhouse; © Oxlock

Printed in China